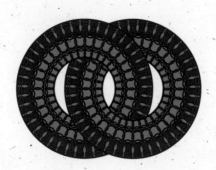

How the Crimes Happened

How the Crimes Happened

POEMS

Dawn Potter

CavanKerry ⟡ Press LTD.

CavanKerry Press Ltd.
Fort Lee, New Jersey
www.cavankerrypress.org

Library of Congress Cataloging-in-Publication Data

Potter, Dawn, 1964-
How the crimes happened / Dawn Potter. – 1st ed.
p. cm.
ISBN-13: 978-1-933880-17-4 (alk. paper)
ISBN-10: 1-933880-17-1 (alk. paper)
I. Title.

PS3616.O8485H69 2009
811'.6–dc22
2009050352

Cover photograph by Thomas Birtwistle

First Edition 2010, Printed in the United States of America

NOTABLE VOICES
CavanKerry ❦ Press

CavanKerry Press is proud to publish the works
of established poets of merit and distinction.

CavanKerry Press is grateful for the support it
receives from the New Jersey State Council on the Arts.

Contents

Contents

III

IV

for Janice, Richard, and Heather,

and in memory of Jilline
(1964–2005)

I

He dilates and exhausts and repeats; he wallows. He is too intent on the passing experience. . . .

He is not thinking of us.

—GEORGE SANTAYANA, ON CHARLES DICKENS (1936)

Radio Song

Clumsy bones, sweet stumbled heart,
  wail your crack-brained tears,
    hunt me in the dark,

shake me blue, crush me in your wire fingers,
  kiss my jagged mouth,
    open me wide,

shove heartbreak through my hundred
  stubborn veins, play me for a fool, I'm so,
    I'm so

unsatisfied, oh clutch my throat,
  cry for me, over and over,
    I bite fingers, I lick salt.

Why I Didn't Finish Reading *David Copperfield*

Bus three's eight-track tape player chunks into gear,
it's Frank Zappa again, crooning huskies and snow,
and down the back of my neck, a couple of bad boys

chant, "Mescaline, peyote, LSD." I've got this book
splayed on my lap, poor Mr. Peggotty, it's not like
I don't feel for him, I just can't keep my mind off

those bony elbows and white hands, those tender,
spotty faces. Glance up in study hall, sure enough,
beautiful bad boys are scrawling "Skynyrd"

all over the chalkboard, the teacher's slipped off
to the supply closet, everyone knows he's got
Mrs. Kay jammed up against a stack of manila paper,

but where is my true love? I worry all the time
I'll end up with nothing, even Barkis-is-willin' won't save me
a smile, I'll be stuck on the bus with Miss Murdstone,

driver shrieking she'll play *The Sound of Music* twice a day
for the rest of the year if those tramps in the backseat
don't keep their hands where she can see them.

I could lay my head on this vinyl seat and cry,
even Little Em'ly has more fun than I do, not one bad boy
in the whole world wants me, I'll never brush my clumsy

lips against his open mouth, taste his sweet smoky breath,
and every time I pick up this book, my mind starts wandering
in circles like an old dog that can't find a good spot to sleep,

you hear his nails clacking back and forth across the kitchen
        floor,
and it just makes me so sad, sitting here on the bus wishing
I was holding hands with a boy in a Kiss t-shirt, my own wild
        Steerforth.

I don't care if he dumps me after a week . . . I don't care.
All I want is to give him everything he asks for, I'd lay myself
        down
in the falling snow to feel the weight of his heart,

and Little Em'ly, if you really needed me, I swear I'd finish
        your story.
Maybe you've floated too long in the cold, or the wind's wrong,
but right now I have no idea what you're screaming about.

Exile

On the morning I left
my country, sunlight

thrust through the clouds
the way it does after a raw

autumn rain, sky stippled
with blue like a young mackerel,

leaf puddles blinking silver,
sweet western wind gusting

fresh as paint, and a flock
of giddy hens rushing pell-mell

into the mud; and I knelt
in the sodden grass and gathered

my acres close, like starched
skirts; I shook out the golden

tamaracks, and a scuffle of jays
tumbled into my spread apron;

I tucked a weary child into each coat
pocket, wrapped the quiet

garden neat as a shroud
round my lover's warm heart,

cut the sun from its moorings
and hung it, burnished and fierce,

over my shield arm—a ponderous
weight to ferry so far across the waste—

though long nights ahead, I'll bless
its brave and crazy fire.

Litany for J

We planned to be old ladies together,
smirking for the camera, cuddled
side by side on a squeaky porch swing,
Alice-and-Gertrude style, modeling

our garden-party housedresses, our pin-
curled hairdos, our rhinestone scuffs.
We planned to marry handsome, good,
educated men capable of fixing broken

lawn mowers *and* discussing the emotional
weight of syntax, men who would grant us
children, freedom, respect, plus
grope us under tables at fancy parties.

We planned to be artists, driven and holy,
greatness flickering in our gut; we meant
to write, speak, sing like angels on moonshine—
like fire, like sin. We planned to prop

and admire, bitch and complain, exaggerate,
gush, tease, and fast-talk, drop literary allusions
like hot tamales, split a bottle of red wine
every night, and whisper rude personal

comments about strangers. We planned
to drink tea at the Plaza, stroll arm in arm
through Central Park, and be accosted

by elderly Armenians in shorts.
We planned to cure cancer through prayer,
dip our irreligious fingers in every holy-water
font in Rome, wear flowered skirts and picture-
frame hats, dissect heartbreak and age, worship

Caravaggio, lose weight, eat fresh tomatoes,
sprawl in the grass, compose sonnets, sing
novelty songs, and wear stiletto heels,
and it took us twenty years, but we crossed

almost everything off our list, yes, we did,
even if our attainments were admittedly half-
assed and fraught with unexpected chickens
flapping home to roost. So who's to say

we won't be sipping a couple of tall g-and-ts
on that swing—you and me, two blue-haired
old ladies, clinking ice cubes, spouting Chaucer,
craving another sack of ripple chips,

whistling Dixie at the fat white moon?
Can't you picture us, large as life
and twice as big? Freshen that lipstick,
darling, brush those chip crumbs off your lap.

Cheek to cheek, now; and blow a kiss to the lens.
This snapshot, it's bound to last forever.

Madrigal

1

What will keep me
        out of this
        bad trouble?
At night, before dawn,
        I picture
        his finger,
reaching slowly
        across his kitchen
        table,
brushing gently,
        gently,
        over my cold knuckles.

2

Does his right hand desire me?
        I watch it now,
        neat, small,
a private hollow.
        Sunlight
        pierces the bright
pages of his book. Words overflow:
        they splash
        our cheeks, our dark lashes
with gold. A glorious
        waste spills
        from our lips.

3

I dream of him
      as a bee accidentally
      dreams of roses.
His wife embraces me tenderly.
      She spreads my clean
      table with white
linen, wine murmurs in the glasses,
      a glim of candle-
      flame
shivers in the small breeze that
      lifts his sad eyes
      to mine.

4

My oven brings forth its brown
      loaves; butter
      glitters in the churn.
There *is* a home for goodness
      in my heart.
      Love feeds there,
like a bird, it scratches a nest of thorn
      and feathers.
      How quietly I wait for him
to come and lean against my ancient walls
      and sing this song that you
      also know so well.

National Emergency

Whosoever travels over this Wilderness
sees it richly bespangled with Evangelical
Churches, blameless emporia, a Hopeful
tangle of high-ways, hamlets, and Smoke.
Americans are the People of God,
the Utmost parts of Earth our Possession.
Soon we shall enjoy *Halcyon* Days,
with all the Vultures of hell
Trodden under our Feet.

Yet a thousand preternatural Things
beyond the Wonders of the former Ages
rise every day before our eyes, and they threaten
a sort of Dissolution upon the World.
The Devil has increas'd a dreadful Knot of *Witches*
in the Country. Spectres inflict our neighbours;
wicked *Scholars* range with their Poisonous
Insinuations among the discontented People.
Publick Safety forces an *Exigency*. To wit:—

Witches are wont to practise their mischievous Facts
by Cursing. Observe the young Mother
wak'd in the Cloudy dawn by her Child's lament.
Does she Leap forth, *Eager* to soothe him at her Bosom?—
or, obstinate and Froward, lie rigid as a Corpse,
pull the heated covers to her chin, and *Curse*
softly, a crafty Decoy to charm her Partner
from his well-earn'd rest and Cheat him
into Stumbling forth?

Some add this for a Presumption:
a mark whereof no evident Reason in Nature
can be given. Consider, now,
the Boy in his first flower, strong and tall,
sprouting, between Darkness and Day,
a *Pimple,* whereof its Exorbitance, like the fires of Baal,
devoureth all joy;—and this Boy,
once clean-temper'd as the Lamb,
doth Erupt in heathen Malice like a *Fiend.*

And here is Evidence of witchcraft:
That the party hath entertain'd a Familiar Spirit,
and had Conference with it, in the likeness
of some visible Creature:
as the Beldame who travels our Holy roads,
a spotted Dog her prancing consort,
suffers him to spew infernal Barks,
raise clamour and complaint,
yet, *without Affliction,* smiles at his Anticks.

Perchance, the suspected person
hath used Enchantments, divineth things
before they come to pass, peremptorily raiseth
Tempests:—judge ye of Weather-men
and Windy commentators; yea, even jug-ear'd
Leaders soaring aloft in Vain glorious Fits.
Says the Devil,
Think thy self better than other Men.
Be some-body.

If the party examin'd be Unconstant,
or contrary to himself, in his deliberate Answers,

this argueth a *Guilty Conscience.*
And yet there are causes of Astonishment
which may befall the Good as well as Bad.
To wrangle the Devil out of the Country
will be truly a New Experiment:—
Unite, then! and lay bare his Thorny
business, therein serving both God and Men.

It is a Principle, that when our Lord permits
Spirits from the unseen Regions to visit us
with surprizing Information, we must enquire.
In our Troubled Sea, Mire and Mud heave up apace.
America is stock'd with Rattle Snakes.
We must Combine to deliver our neighbours
from the horrid Annoyances of witchcraft.
We are *Safe,* when we make Perfect use
of Invisible Advice, as God proffers it.

Manilow Fan

"Is it true?—is it really true? Is Barry
huge back east?" begs the twelve-year-old
girl in the "Barry" hat answering the knock

of an earnestly hungover Greenpeace canvasser
originally planning to tap into his standard
manifesto on harp seals, Monsanto, and the awesome

bullying powers of the *Rainbow Warrior;* now trapped,
thunderstruck and tongue-tied, on this freezing
doorstep in Edina, Minnesota, overcome by vibrations

that might be the fault of last night's tequila
but feel like a fireworks blast of unsubstantiated news:
a vision of the northeast decked out as Gargantua's

Copa, rhinestones glittering from fire escapes, golden
showgirls high-stepping through glitter-lit trails in the dirty
snow; and there, rubbing shoulders with the Empire State

like a smooth King Kong, it's Barry the Man himself,
stretching forth a slim white hand, tossing his shiny hair,
ready to belt out the song that makes the whole world sing,

even, for a second, this part-time do-gooder
emerging from his daze on a stoop in Minnesota,
still primed to tell Barry's little fan, "Hey,

Manilow's the greatest; he's a sensation everywhere!"
though he suspects the right thing to do
is to break the news that "this is the 80s, kid.

Punk rockers drink in the bar around the corner.
Get with the times"; and the truth is that "Mandy"
is, like, his least favorite song ever; so the question is,

What's the spirit of Barry doing here, stuck in a time warp
on this grim suburban plain? No doubt, the girl could
explain it all; he'd like to plunk down on her shoveled steps

and let her show him exactly how the Barry magic
works; but something stops him, a sort of awkward
muzzling of wonder, like when smack in the middle

of a long wet kiss, you sneeze: and instantly
every trace of romance bursts like a blister
and the angel you'd been about to die for

tucks in her shirt and decides to go to class;
and what he ends up doing in Edina
is to rub his cold nose against his splintery

clipboard, scuff his Sandinista boots
on the Vikings welcome mat, and mutter,
"Uh, I don't know. . . . Is your mom home?"

Heavy Metal

With what care you compromise your righteous taste
      for noise in service to your rampant sons;
      linger like a pirate over Goodwill bins, the waste
of wretched yard sales, sifting one by one

the halt, the lame; then slip into the kitchen
      after dark, kiss my shoulder, unload groceries,
      pour a second beer, and, offhand, think to mention
you've just purchased our first-ever AC/DC

record. You!—dear secret and embarrassed owner
      of Boston, Wings, and K-Tel disco albums,
      derider of Pete Seeger and the Weavers, stalwart hater
of the Beach Boys, despiser of dull stoner jams—

      you closet Modern Lover, not forgetting that a young
      boy needs to shake his ravished parents all night long.

Eclogues

Look, oxen now bring home their yoke-suspended ploughs,
And the sun, going down, doubles growing shadows;
But I burn in love's fire: can one set bounds to love?

—VIRGIL

1

The lovage is the shade
of Lincoln green in Sherwood,
stealthy green, its leaves sharp-tongued
and leathery and rude.

Even in the garden it is safe
from fortune hunters, its display
of riches cool and well restrained,
like yours today.

All hints I send to you are wrong,
misheard, or undergone
in tears. Long for me again.
Pour out your crazy thrush's song,

screel a hawk's lament three times,
or drum a grouse-beat in the pines.
Then in the lovage, hide your sign,
buried in the leaves, near mine.

2

A marriage worth of minutes we've stood
side by side, staring into the hooded depths
of your 1984 Dodge Ram pickup truck,
watching the engine chitter and die
for no apparent reason. I feel a crazy,
ignorant joy: here we go again, sweetheart,
struggling in harness over yet another
crappy mystery. Do you? I can't say I'll ever
know one way or the other what your thoughts
will do, though twenty years ago I made you cry
when I dumped you for the jerk down the hall,
and I'll never get over it, the sight of you,
cool autocrat, in tears for a dumb girl
who happened to be me.

Now I'm the one who cries all the time,
you're the one not walking away from me
down the hall. Just the same, you imagine
walking away, I'm sure of it; maybe when you're
dragging another snow-sopped log to the chainsaw
pile, or we're curled in bed waiting for a barred owl
to stammer in the pines, the barn dog shouting back
like a madwoman. It's not that being here
is misery; it's more like marriage is too much
and not enough at the same time: the trees crowd us
like children, our bodies betray a fatal longing.
What's left for us, at forty, but dismay
till labor shakes us back into our yoke.

Work, work, that puritan duty—yet
how beautiful the set of your shoulders
when you heave a scrap of metal siding
into the trash heap. Our bodies linger
this side of lovely, like flowers under glass.
We drive ourselves to endure; on my knees
in the hay mow, stifled and panting,
I plant bale after bale in place: you toss,
you toss, I shove, I shove. We keep pace,
patient and wordless; the goats in their pen
blat irritably. In the yard our sons quarrel.
Mourning doves groan in the eaves.
Long hours ahead, till our job is done
and another begins.

Hunting scattered chickens in the bug-infested dew:
I watch you crouch along the scrubby poplar edge,
then circle back between the apple trees,
white hen skittering ahead, luminescent in the shabby
dark. Suddenly she drops her head and sits,
submissive as a girl. You've got her now; tuck up her feet
and carry her back home, then squat to mend the ragged
        fence.
A breath of sweat rises from your sunburnt neck,
salt and sweet. My love. Marry me, I say. You cast
an eye askance and shrug, I did. How odd it seems
that this is where we've landed: chasing chickens
through the woods at twilight, humid thunder rumpling
the summer sky, dishes washed, a slice of berry pie left
cooling on the counter. I've been saving it for you.

3

All the long day, rain
pours quicksilver
down the blurred glass.
Gardens succumb to forest,

half-ripe tomatoes cling
hopelessly to yellow vines,
cabbages crumple and split,
but who cares?

Let summer vanish,
let the tired year
shrink to the width
of a cow path,

soppy hens straggle
in their narrow yard,
and every last leaf
on the maples redden,

shrivel, and die.
Nothing needs me,
today, but you,
sweet hand,

cupping the bones
of my skull. Alas,
poor Yorick, picked clean
as an egg.

How rich we grow,
bright sinew and blood,
my eyes open, yours
blue.

4

Play "Sister Morphine" four or five times an hour,
sleet jittering the window, and what is it about that song

yanking the chain so tight I have to cover my eyes
before walls collapse? A lover can set bounds to love,

but then, is it still love, or some kinder emotion?
Trollope's married ladies esteem their ample lords;

but look at crazy Bradley Headstone, he doesn't
esteem Lizzie one bit, though he loves her

like a man from hell.
The novels say I'm reaching the prime of life

when I ought to forget about skin by firelight,
but I've always been a sucker for desire, I can't stop now

just because my friends have marriageable daughters.
Girls these days, they don't grow up watching Virginia

Woolf stir the soup, Juliet behind the barn dying for love.
What girl wants to be Virginia-thinking-of-Juliet anymore?

You're stuck with me, dear boy, pockets full of rocks,
though at least the river's frozen, no drownings till spring.

You'll have to give up the ghost and let me love you;
it's the best I can do, this dark age.

II

You can always tell old people's music. It's louder than ours.

—ELEVEN-YEAR-OLD BOY, ON WHY HE HATES THE WHO (2004)

Substitute Teacher

after Elizabeth Bowen

You look at places
you are leaving,
thinking: What
did I hope to find?–

a ten-year-old
fat girl alight
in the fluorescent
shimmer of Monday

fear, blank field
beyond a window
gray as a mitten,
a stack of syllables

against your tongue,
savage and unkempt–
here, in the emptiest
room on this round

earth: a slew of eyes,
blackbird bright,
and your thin
hands, mouthing air–

a single note,
ticking, ticking . . .
a vast alarm
of silence.

First Game

Late winter afternoon. The gym bleachers are stuffed
not quite shoulder to shoulder with heavy-set
mothers and fathers, parkas unlashed, tired haunches

roosting on the narrow benches. Walking babies zip
ponderously back and forth along the footways, clutching
soggy Fig Newtons. Eighth-grade girls cluster in a corner,

sucking up Mountain Dew and trying on each other's shoes.
Hot little boys bounce up and down like basketballs,
wishing they *were* basketballs, or basketball stars,

or their older brothers, or dragons. The hot little boys
shoot out loud dreams like BBs, bouncing up and down
incessantly, and the walking babies briefly quit

zipping and bounce up and down companionably,
and the girls in the corner suddenly scatter, inserting
themselves into tight spots next to their parents

or scooping up a walking baby and squeezing her till
she burps and drops her wet cookie onto her father's boot.
Like poltergeists, two eighth-grade boys materialize

on the gym floor wearing whistles. The rumor flies:
Nate and Scott are the refs! Sheepishly, the refs pop
layups, and the eighth-grade girls snicker sardonically.

The hot little boys clap and bounce up and down
and blow ear-splitting solos on invisible whistles. The girls
drop the babies and regroup in the corner, smirking

and confabulating. And now the walking babies
shriek, "Bubby!" because here they come,
the seven fifth- and sixth-grade boys of the Harmony School

B-team basketball squad, running heel to heel, full tilt,
circling the outside foul line, glossy blue-and-white uniforms
fluttering from their narrow shoulders, rosy faces glowing,

skinny legs pumping, fluorescence sparking off bent eyeglasses:
and it's thrilling and sad and beautiful and painfully sweet:
it's the Charge of the Light Brigade, and the crowd's chatter

shivers into silence because, at such moments, a parent's
throat aches too much to cheer. It's pride they feel,
but also sorrow, and loneliness, watching their red-cheeked

sons dash so recklessly away in their bright tunics
like they're galloping toward the horizon.
The moment trembles, fragile as sea-foam, and then

crashes and fades when the Athens B-team thunders in
from the boys' bathroom and the Athens parents
on the other side of the gym let out their ordinary

whoops and howls, and the Harmony cavalry
recedes into a clutter of benched eleven-year-olds
slurping Gatorade, poking each other in the ribs,

and surreptitiously waving at their mothers.
On the floor, the starters fling foul shots in a hiatus
of peaceful chaos, the refs slink into corners

to try out their whistles, the crowd relaxes into vagary
until the janitor honks the buzzer, the walking babies
yelp, and the season opener erupts:

And in these first seconds, every non-baby in the gym
understands that the Harmony B-team is doomed.
Like a covey of bewildered little partridges, or Pickett's boys

innocently galumphing up a Gettysburg ridge,
our players stumble face-first into slaughter.
They fumble every pass, dribble on their ankles,

aim layups two feet below the backboard, congregate
helplessly under the basket as a fat Athens booby
nails yet another three-pointer; and even the refs'

incompetent favors can't save them. The little boys
in the bleachers scowl in star-struck disbelief,
and jaded grandparents mutter, "These boys

gotta get *tough*." Packed together in their corner,
the eighth-grade girls shout, "Idiots! Steal the ball!"
and "Oh my God, you suck!" and in that instant

an alarm, a buffalo instinct, ripples among the parents:
an obstinate, unspoken urge to circle their hapless calves,
and though the girls in the corner keep broadcasting

their brothers' ineptness, and the hot little boys
bad-mouth the scoreboard, and the walking babies
wail because they can't have the ball,

the Harmony mothers and fathers square their feet,
shift their heavy shoulders, and do what needs to be done:
They radiate a stream of loyal affection so dense and united

that the very air begins to smell of love—
not just for their own sons, but for every clumsy, familiar
body on the floor, for every boy who ever built Lego racecars

on their carpet or dug for gold in their driveway, for every
        Scout
who sold them bad popcorn or collected their Coke cans,
for every pain in the ass they ever yelled at to stop

jumping on the beds—and it billows through the gym, this
        love,
like a spring mist, or maybe laughing gas, and our boys
panting on the floor glance up at their parents, goggle-eyed,

dog-like in their relief. They would not be amazed
to witness their tired fathers stomping onto the court
in mechanics' pants and workboots and barricading

the Athens huns in the storage room until the Harmony boys
can even up the score. It's not that they're expecting this
        miracle.
But love is a solace, though no one in the gym dreams

of speaking those words. The players are minutes
into their first game, and already everyone has forgotten
their glory. The hot little boys expound on good ideas

for squelching opponents, such as glue and trip wires. Babies
hiccup and suck dirt off their fingers, but mothers and fathers
salute every single happiness they see, even after one son

bounces a pass off another's head, even after a third son
carefully hands the ball to an Athens guard like a birthday
cake. So when Nate the ref finally figures out how to blow

his whistle and his accidental shriek echoes off the D.A.R.E
posters like a supersonic train wreck, Harmony cheers
to beat the band. The game's already a lost cause,

but joy matters. The parents shift their weight on the hard
benches and pull wet babies onto their knees. The girls
chant, "Whis-tle, whis-tle. . . ." Athens swishes a second

foul shot. And those lead-foot boys in blue
lurching hopelessly after the loose ball?
Don't worry. They belong to us.

Touching

at school is against the rules,
so when a spike-haired

first grader in need
butts up against your hip,

don't you wrap your arms
round his skinny bones, don't you

cup his skull in your palms,
smooth a knuckle up his baby cheek:

he's got lice, he's got AIDS;
you kiss him, you die,

or worse: late nights, he'll hunch up small,
stare into some laugh show

and whisper what no half-pissed dad
cares to hear from his wife's

kid at the end of a long day
of nothing, when sleep

is the only country,
anywhere else, terror:

a father you've marked
before, slouching into parent night,

two hands trembling
along his thighs like birds

shot down,
black eyes wary as a bull's:

he blinks at the butcher,
you smile, you fold

your unheld hands;
what roils in his wake is the one

you won't teach
to beg an answer from love.

Cornville

*Let us discuss why poetry has lost the power of making men
brave.*
—E. M. FORSTER

In front of every third house is a for-sale lineup
not of corn but of flat-bellied pumpkins and warty
hubbards tinted that improbable robin's-egg blue,
also butternuts, tediously beige, and turk's heads
that look like Turk's heads, though the sales clincher

among these hopeful come-hithers is surely the "PUM
PKINS" sign, a squat two-line exhortation spray-painted
onto a square board and stabbed into a scruff of weeds.
But Jill's son won't let her stop the car, not even for pum
pkins; he claims this cheerful roadside merchandise

"might not be good enough," though he refuses to elaborate
because he's concentrating on Joe Castiglione, Voice
of the Boston Red Sox, who's executing a thrilling on-air
play-by-play fit over the alacritous mouse careening
across his shoes in the Tropicana Field press box;

yet even in mid-fluster the intrepid Voice manages
to recount a few pertinent clubhouse-mouse anecdotes,
for who can forget (intones the Voice) the great Phil Rizzuto,
whose severe mouse hate occasionally tempted a bored
Yankee to park a dead rodent in his fielder's glove?

Her son, alert and unamazed, sucks up this radio tumult
like oxygen; and if he's more exercised by Rizzuto's
shortstop stats than by the image of a long-suffering
Trop Field janitor stowing a poised and baited trap
between the Voice's jittery feet, it's merely a symptom

of his ascetic attention, the rich curiosities of discipline
he's imposed on his brain, where details of mouse fear
are mere decorative flourishes in the noble history
of baseball—this unfurling seasonal pageant of power
and beauty and earnest fidelity among a pack of heroes

who can't possibly blow their seven-game lead,
can they? Another pumpkin stage-set flashes past Jill
on this Cornville road where, come to think of it,
there *was* corn once, and not so many days ago either:
acres of it, bobbing green and ostrich-like over these mild
        foothills,

but now shaved close, row upon row of dun-colored stubble
fading to dirt, the harvest's backward march to blankness,
an oracular patriarch reverting to beardless boy—
mouse heaven, no doubt, but not a modern paradise
the like of Tropicana Field, vast echoing hall of crumbs,

home of Cracker Jack galore and brisk secret scrambles
among an eternity of folding chairs. That poor radio
adventurer scampering over the Voice's shiny feet:
he's a goner, no question about it, bound to be trap-snapped,
maybe this at-bat or the next, for the Voice will not forbear,

no extra innings for rodents, and Jill herself cannot abide mice,
those Sisyphean wretches shoving rocks back and forth, back
and forth, all night above her bedroom ceiling; she lies awake,
rigid and furious, wishing them dead. The roadside unrolls
like a backdrop; Jill's car swallows tarmac, smoothly, greedily;

yes, Cinderella's godmother magicked pumpkins into coaches,
mice into footmen; but can a princess trust a mouse-man
not to steal her shiny slippers and stuff them under a garret
floorboard? Or does she lie in bed, night after night,
listening to the Voice chatter and complain on the prince's

kitchen radio, to the mouse-man scuffle and creak
above her head? Is she wishing him dead?
Jill's son, like any prince, is indifferent to the mouse,
though also magnanimous, though also ruthless.
The mouse doesn't gnaw at him. A princess

is different—touchier, guiltier. Peter, Peter, pumpkin eater,
had a wife but couldn't keep her, and no wonder—
they fret so, these wives and princesses, not like the Voice,
who takes a break from his mouse to sell a few Volvo safety tips
and discuss the fine backyard sheds available for purchase

at Home Depot. In the backseat Jill's son chortles lustily
alongside a Kubota jingle . . . Put her in a pumpkin shell
and there he kept her very well, and what on earth
is that supposed to mean? These nursery rhymes:
they're like the Good Book—nothing but hint, trickery, or
    truth.
Jill glances up at the Harley swelling into rear mirror view

and thinks about ire and anti-Peter feminists and pulpit-
        pounding
preachers and screaming Big Papi fans, and sighs,
not because she's necessarily immune to energetic belief, or
        even
energetic hope: but it's tiresome, this inability to gracefully

tolerate a riddle. We forget the Sphinx and gape at Oedipus;
nothing consoles our lost honor. If the Red Sox
blow the series, her son will weep noisily into his banner,
betrayed, aghast–not exactly implying that Beowulf
died in battle so why shouldn't Manny Ramirez

brain himself with a bat instead of shrugging "Better luck
next time," but really: what does *brave* require?
Not falling on your sword after losing to the Devil Rays
but maybe not "if a bully bothers you on the playground,
just walk on by," even if the second version comforts

those son-loving mothers who aren't Grendel's:
though it would be easy enough to be Grendel's mother,
Jill thinks suddenly, grieving and vengeful, loping savagely
from her hole in the fens, wretched, livid, desperately hungry
for Danes; and she's startled at the vision, for it can be
        strangely

tonic to picture oneself as a monster, especially at moments
of maternal docility, child strapped safely in the backseat
of a well-airbagged automobile, robust squash glinting in the
        autumn
sunlight, sky as clean and blue as a morning glory, a sedate

Harley-with-sidecar tooling up behind her. Properly blinking,
the bike passes her; and as it rumbles by her window,
she catches sight of the oversized Rottweiler
wedged into the sidecar. He looks like Stonehenge
on the run, head thick as a brick, little ears aflutter,
yawp gaping with delight and solidly drooling

into the wind. He looks, come to think of it,
like Big Papi heading home for lobster after a cheerful
ball-chasing afternoon, a man who (according to her son)
named his kid after a sub shop, surely a Rottweiler
token of happiness, for there's a certain plain bravery in joy;

and imagine those golden-haired Geats, shields glinting,
splashing up the stony beach—late-day sun, a sea of spears
and shadows; even a mouse owns the courage
of his enchantments; and how the Voice loves his voice,
the quick syllables, the straining verbs, the fervor of the tale—

"He *crushed* that pitch," exclaims the Voice; and meanwhile,
a mouse considers a peanut-laced trap; meanwhile, Jill's car
trails a disappearing fat dog down a twisting Cornville avenue;
meanwhile, her son suddenly falls asleep against his window,
his mind blossoming with heroes, except that all of them

are himself, everything, yes, everything, depends on his quick
and powerful blow, and how these bright standards
fly in the wind as the men gather in the broad meadow,
a host of warriors, raising their heavy goblets
to salute the king.

The Master

Leo's eleven, but he still can't write "Leo."
He throws a pencil at me.
"*You* write the poem," he says.
He frowns and leans back in his chair

and shuts his eyes.
In the flat autumn light, his glasses
shed a watery glow. His freckles tremble.
Leo always likes to keep me waiting.

After a minute he growls,
"Big heifers in the corn again,
And them horses
Is hungry."

After a minute he snarls,
"Coyote snitched the rawhide.
Grab a gun and blast him,
Then skin him up."

Twenty other kids breathe hard,
scribble, and erase. Danyell chews
on the end of a pen and sighs gustily.
"Can I make this up?" she complains.

Leo slouches and crosses his arms
over his bony ribs. He opens his eyes
and smiles in a superior manner.
In his view, imagination sucks.

What matters in a poem
is you tell it like it happened
but you leave out the crap.
He jerks his chin up,

looks me over, slitty-eyed. He says,
"*I* do something *I* do it right!"
When that bell screams,
he's number one out the door.

Violin Recital

Humming box of echoes, satin
    frame twitching under the child's grasp
        like a docile rabbit,
            quivering, alive; taut

silver purling call-and-response,
    torqued gut and ebony potent
        as storm, more
            secret than air,

primed innocence, parting
    naked lips for the coloratura
        oath dragged forth
            bow and scrape, a terrible

roar toward glory—
    reckless, infant—weltering under a high-
        wire apogee, gypsy fingers
            crowding the steep,

hunger quaking, prowling, through floorboards,
    knees, through nervous hips,
        hands slick with sweat, pricked ear
        canny as a bitten fox.

Diner

You fall into your window seat like a stork
spearing an alewife, my little cabbage,

and you eat so much cabbage! Chatter
harrows the fog-lit air. I wad napkins with spilt milk,

socks explode from your rat-tail shoes,
you suck two straws and snicker Farty Mart,

but when you have nothing else to say,
you say, I love you, Mom,

more times an hour than I can bear.
Oh my sweetheart, my barometer,

my wet-nose calf, my chick—
I grimace at a sudden knife of sun, you kick my chair

and bellow, What's wrong?
early-alert system, wired and ready,

grubby hackles spiked,
bitten fingernail held to the wind.

Moo a tune, you can't fool me.
I hear you:

Look out, a big one's brewing, batten the hatches,
I love you, Mom,

I'm ducking my head,
I love you, Mom, I'm ready to run.

Peter Walsh

1

One might make a start today, *this* day, to tell the story of a life.
For a life must begin somewhere. Peter Walsh was his name;
and someone had written that name in thick white ink
beneath the image of a child in short pants who looked down
at his cupped hands, and in his hands sat an egg;

a goose egg, was it? or perhaps the egg of a large duck,
or perhaps simply a hen's egg in a small boy's hands?
And behind him, was the sea rolling? or was it a field of ripe
hay? And why had someone dropped a spotted scarf at his feet?
In the doorway, his mother tormented herself with dust and
     disarray:

yes, look at these photographs, waxy with dirt; piano filthy
as coal. And yet there was Peter. And yet there was herself.
A mother brings forth a child and calls him by name;
but what, in the story of his life, does her travail signify?
Merely nothing, perhaps. A signpost to wander away from.

Curtains spoke to wind; a fly complained. The parlor was
     empty
now but not silent. The kitchen intruded: click of china, rattle
     of steel.
Voices. On the pianoforte the snapshots smiled, or did not,
each fenced in its solitary room: once he was this age; then
he was that tall. His mother had scattered them with no
     particular intent.

She rarely saw them, for she saw her child every day as he was.
He rarely saw them, for as documents they had no meaning.
They were objects only, settled on the piano as dust also
settled there. Sometimes they shivered, gently, when Peter
struck the keys. But he did not watch them tremble.

2

One might make a start today, *this* day, to tell the story of a life.
For a life must begin somewhere, birth or otherwise,
and Peter's life (as much as he thought of it) might thus far
have never begun at all, except as explained by its regalia
of framed smiles and comic punch lines, the shabby

trousers and terse adventures trapped in the snapshots
lining the dusty pianoforte (the soft-loud, he named it in his
  mind,
and sometimes he struck out the words, *soft-loud-soft-loud*
on the stained keys, like a password or an incantation,
for no one else seemed to notice them at all, these sounds

distracting him, sucking him away from the nothingness
of childhood: of chewing rhubarb and running haywire
across a stubbled field, of pissing against a tree and watching
his own hot stain leak down the bark runnels, quenching the
  dirt).
One might call life a tale of noticing: a span of intensities,

moments when we suddenly attend to eye or hand or ear;
more, they exact our attention, like an internal command:
Now you are alive. On the pianoforte Peter struck out the words

soft-loud-soft-loud in a sort of dream idleness,
fingertips against keys, muscles contracting, each pitch,

each duration, a subtle, unintended chant, and all the while
bees shimmered in the bright air outside the pocked
window, motes danced in the streaks of sunlight resting
like calm hands on the chairs and carpets, and Peter
lived it all, lived everything: in the parlor, in the unseen

rooms beyond, in the long, low gardens stretching
toward field and forest; and yet he lived none of it:
for life, the richness of earth, sought him out,
claimed his open eye, his voluntary ear, as he lingered
at the piano, striking *soft-loud-soft-loud* on the stained keys,

idle and untutored, shirttail thrust into his frayed
belt, a smear of green willow on the seat of his shorts.
In the kitchen his mother half heard his *plink-plonk-
plink-plonk;* more, she felt it, like a tremor, an emanation,
safe and dull as a drip down a drainpipe:

a comfort, in truth; for now and then she faced
the facts of tedium with a sort of satisfaction,
a release from this ever-lasting hunt for bliss
that seemed, to her surprise, to have been her task
all these years of her life: chasing down the next

thing and the next, and was it squalor or success,
her plans for dinner and the garden and the fruits
of her own mind? She half heard Peter's *plink-plonk*
and half felt the chimes of her own future clang
in step, then out of step with his idle fingers, uneven

as a ticking clock on a crooked shelf. On the porch
rail two jays sparred; new potatoes bubbled on the stove;
she was making salad, her hands tore lettuce; her hands
were red and worn; they were her grandmother's hands.
How strange! She watched her grandmother's hands tear

lettuce, the jays quarreled on the railing; a sparrow
cried, *Oh, Sam Peabody, Peabody, Peabody;* Peter played
two notes on the piano, and would he ever stop, would
they ride on and on forever, two notes clanging in the summer
air? It was unbearable, and she cried out, *Stop it! If you're*

going to play the piano, play a song, for God's sake!
and at the sound of her voice, the notes crumpled up
on themselves and vanished, as if they had never lived at all,
as if there were no such notes in the history of the world.
Somewhere a screen door snapped open, and shut.

3

Peter never thought to love his mother less because she
interrupted these small commas, these accidental
obsessions, which were not knowledge but merely time
stopped in its tracks, no more vital than sleep. His bicycle lay
on its flank in the dooryard, dead as a shot horse; he scooped
    it up,

he shook it back to life; he mounted and cantered down
the ragged lawn: sedate robins burst into flight, horrified;
he drove the bicycle harder, grinding into mole holes, through
    humps

of weed; wind snatched at his hair; the bicycle lurched and
    galloped
under his hands and the forest rose up from the distance

and became tangles and trunks and shadow, and with a
    flourish
of tire, Peter pulled up his horse and threw it to the ground
and threw himself onto his back beside it and stared at the clouds,
which leapt in the air like starlings and swallows, until his eyes
shut of their own accord and he stared at the magic swirls

behind his eyelids that also leapt like birds, and it was not sleep,
not at all like sleep, but like gangster movies, in a way; and also
like getting sick on the merry-go-round; but it didn't matter,
nothing mattered: there was not one thing more important
in this world than another, unless it was his knife, which had

three dull blades and a fold-out spoon. One might make a start
today, this day, to tell the story of a life; yet a life is the story
of nothing, the story of Peter on his back in the grass,
squirming a hand into the right hip pocket of his shorts,
curling his hand around the hidden lump of knife

that his mother had given him for his tenth birthday;
and nothing ever happened because of it: he never
killed anything with this knife; he never even cut himself;
and when he was sixteen, riding a wooden roller coaster
with his cousin, it fell out of his pocket, vanished into the salty

mud, and he never missed it, not once, for the rest of his life;
but a life is also the story of noticing just now, just at this
    moment,

what we never notice again: and just now the knife lay curled
in Peter's palm and he caressed it blindly, with thumb and
    palm
and fingertip; he lay with his eyes closed and leaf-speckled
    sunlight

stippling his cheeks. A life is the story of nothing, yet once a
    watcher
believed a moment meant something more than nothing,
believed in the story of a child named Peter Walsh. It began,
that story, and ended, and no one ever knew what became of
    him,
the child who carried an egg in his hands, beside the sea.

Don't be afraid to

lug a fat kid into rain, laugh when his mouth
flaps opens like a chick's, stumble south
through weary dumps and truck-torn
roads, past autumn gnats who mourn
at Greaney's turkey farm, where redcoats
sling up roosters heel by heel, slit throats,

drain hearts, while maples twist an eye-
blue sky, a rush of wild geese swings by:
good enough day to kill or die,
perch shivering on a tailgate, fly.

III

What matter where, if I still be the same?

—JOHN MILTON, ON SATAN (1667)

The Fall

The Fiend thought of the Stairs as a sort of emergency ladder
descending from the firmament like Rapunzel's braid,
mysterious and glittering, and only occasionally useful
(since God yanked them up as the spirit moved him),
though when operational they worked more or less
like an escalator, sweeping swarms of pintucked angels
grandly into the celestial ballroom, for who would expect
angels to climb hand over hand up a hairy ladder,
panting and sweating like ordinary princes?
At the marge of the Stairs lapped an opalescent sea,
a gulf of liquid pearl, each wave as sluggish as polenta
on the boil, and over it sailed alabaster barges weighed down
with seraphim on tour, though, as he might have expected,
no one waved when he coasted by. For some reason
God had let down the Stairs that day, whether to dare
his enemy to easy ascent or to aggravate his sad exclusion
from the party, who could tell? But as it happened,
the Fiend had other fish to fry.

For the Stairs descended, through a film of sea,
to that playhouse of angels, Earth, toy paradise of trees
and fruit and docile tigers, patient as sleep beneath the slow
ocean ripple; and the Fiend, folding his wings and halting
at the fulcrum of the golden Stairs scaling both Heaven and
        Earth,
looked with wonder at the sudden view of all this world,
like a climber who bursts from a gnarled, branchy darkness
to find, at one instant, the map of the forest spread before
        him–

a feast of lakes, rivers, sun-struck glades—and above him
the sky, the sky, the sky! And at sight of such beauty,
the Fiend was seized by joy and discontent, heartrending
in near equal portion, and was stymied for a moment
from his purpose, despite his malice, lingering to scrutinize
the canopy of shade and light, until, with some reluctance,
he shook out his heavy wings and leaped down
through the slow-running sea, down the broad Stairs
toward Earth, falling like Alice through the pure air, past star
after star, bright island worlds, though he never paused
to ask who dwelt there in such happy ignorance.

Burglar

A green taloned hedge, so massive
      a dove could not flutter over, so dense
an armored snake could not slip beneath—
      This was the obstacle
between the Fiend and earthly delight!
      Thin-hipped, high-shouldered,
chin in hand, he studied the situation.
      Of course, far on the other side
of the Garden, due east, there was a gate,
      if he chose to hike the border and rap
on the front door. What the Fiend
      puzzled over, at the moment,
was not the trouble of getting in,
      which for an angel was minimal,
but this curious pretense of a barricade—
      Why make it so fraught yet convenient
to break into a park that, no matter how
      buxom, was merely a dull facsimile of bliss?
This was the kind of setup that had always
      irritated him—the King's cunning
propensity for dramatic ambiguity, "free will"
      with a catch, not to mention
these ridiculous processional formalities.
      "Ugh," muttered the Fiend;
and with a contemptuous snap of his wings
      at one slight bound he leaped over the hedge,
landing on his feet as briskly as a cat
      dropping through a henhouse window
into a huddle of fat chicks.

Then up he flew, up to the middle tree,
the highest that grew in the yard, and perched,
     kneecaps tucked to his ears,
black as a cormorant in the frilled branches;
     and there he devised his next really good idea.

The Fiend's Soliloquy

O Hell!
The truth is I leaked tears
the instant I laid eyes on you, my idle pair
of babes, plump as pomegranates,
sporting with your lions and tigers and such:
Only clay and water, I'm sure, but so realistic!—
all those wanton ringlets and kissable folds . . .
Well, any fool might mistake you for angels,
and I, though unfoolish,
admit a penchant for pretty faces
and a miracle. How ever does He do it?
Always, my thoughts pursue that wonder,
and you, mirror of my wonder,
you also they chase:
Why conceal it?
I could love you.

So shall I say
I'm sorry the wind has shifted
and grim winter lurks in the east?
Let me be frank, my doves:
Shall I, unpitied, pity you—
gathering your melons and rosebuds,
licking up your milky dregs of delight?
Call it love, if you prefer, but I *will* have you.
Does it cheer you to know
that likewise you will have me?
In the evening by the fire,
how we will argue, our shabby children

scampering amok among the ashes!
Poor chucks, should I,
at your silly sweetness, melt?
    Well, I do. But too bad.

Eve's Dream

Not of your sweet wandering hands, nor even
of yesterday's seed or tomorrow's green pear,
but of crime and trouble, yes, offenses that never

crossed my fancy before this wretched night:
for in my dreams a quiet voice at my ear
coaxed me awake; and I thought it was you

cajoling me into the pleasant shadows,
cool and silent, save when silence yields
to cricket scratch or throaty owl,

white moon-face waxing gibbous
and all the Heavens awake in their glory
though none else to revel in them but ourselves;

and I rose and walked out into the night,
but where were you? I called your name,
then ventured, restive, into the lunar

garden I knew so well by day, yet here
I lost myself in white light and black hole,
I staggered through puddles, over stones;

and I heard, in my heartbeat,
an invisible horror, I heard it tease me,
chase me, catch me; and I ran, I ran,

weeping I ran; until, under moonglow,
I saw my own pale hands stretch before me
toward the Tree that blocked my way;

I saw my hands embrace it, caress its satin skin.
And in return, the Tree kissed my captive lips
with its feathery leaves, as if a twist of wind

had leagued us suddenly together;
for it gleamed strange and terrible,
this great rooted flower,

plying me so gently with Knowledge:
though my lips, parched and ravenous,
begged, now, for a rougher, a crueler dram.

IV

Dawn . . . is the most usual time for men to be carried off by fever.

—ROBERT GRAVES, ON THE GREEK GODDESS EOS (1955)

Aubade

And what about the small eye, Walter?–
the leaves of grass you overlooked, winter
lichen clutching fence posts, a draggled
dead squirrel in the snowbank, the red
letters of my name, serif by slant?
It was bliss you sighed, panted,

howled for: the View from Space—
big comet Walt chasing Madam Eos
across a streaky sky, old guilty dawn
tempting another kosmic shaman
to lurch word-drunk from the rafters . . .
oh, I grieve for every morning-after

groan rising from your sallow bed
as I fire your cookstove, bake your bread.

Last Day

In mourning the parakeet props his blue wings
     awry, sourly fluffs his feathers; with a sort
of Willy Loman resignation he hunches his short
     neck, his frail shoulders. Days past, he would sing

backup to any tune—the smoke alarm, the White
     Stripes, erupt into an avian scat solo, wild child
of cool, jazz messenger from the bestiary side.
     Now anyone can tell he'll be dead before night

sifts down through these overripe maples, this sweet
     mosquito gloaming: slit eye plunging fathoms
through an empty sea, pale breast a shallow cavern
     of farewell, each tiny gasp a plummet

into dark; yet how long he takes to die!—death
killing pity even as it covets his brief, failing breath.

Rumpelstiltskin's Garden

Rain, and more rain! And now
this whore sunshine!
Grass, how dare you inflict yourself

on my desires, you and your weed-
sprung clan, shattering the peonies,
raping the barren hops.

Filthy mess of life!
You thrive for spite,
like the princeling who squalls in the muddy

shadows, like the miller's queen
shedding ice in my heart's parlor.
Fury! Fury!

I could tear myself in two,
sever like stove wood under the axe,
then split again a thousand times,

pound myself to ash
till all the busy ants in christendom
couldn't sort my rage from dust.

Protestant Cemetery

Here lies one whose name was writ in water.

Keats is dead, time's swift apprentice
tramping the grimy London lanes,
pockets crammed with pencil stubs, two mice,
a half-penned letter of delight—"ah!
had I never known your kindness . . ."

and Shelley is dead, one white hand
clutching a tinker-toy mast,
silk scarf flying, a torrent of curls
shock-whipped by wind, and the sea
tearing sheets from her bed;

and baby Severn is dead, reckless
philosopher of floors and stairwells,
founder of speech, tyrant-prince,
squawking cricket, famished
at twilight and dawn;

and here they lurk, next door to a squatty
pyramid, ten or twelve feral cats, a flea market
packed with bargain-mad nuns; and before us,
a whistling man digging a ditch. Two pear-shaped
English ladies consult a guidebook,

peering anxiously at a laurel shrub
for aid; the cheerful digger, unconsulted,
flaps a dirty hand toward the damp corner

where Keats and baby Severn hide,
not far from baby Shelley,

though Shelley himself is stuffed into denser
congress, cheek-to-jowl with Corso,
that misbegotten seeker, and a thousand other
amputated poets, Christian soldiers, wastrel
lovers of light not cited in the ladies' guidebook

or anywhere else, for that matter,
a collection of forgotten Protestants farmed out
for eternity to this heretic Anglo-Saxon outpost
nestled at the bony knee of an ancient dump,
by far the tidiest park I've seen in Rome.

Compare the Aventine on Sunday morning—
parade of chubby brides and crabby mothers,
grooms dangling like haute-couture chimps
from the orange trees, high-heeled grandmas
shaking fists at pig-headed husbands who refuse

to beam, a dozen stray soccer balls, bums snoring
in the lanky grass, and beyond us, all Rome
painted under the haze like a tacky postcard.
They don't let bums nap in the Protestant Cemetery,
though it would be a pleasant place to rest,

like sleeping in the Secret Garden, high-walled
and remote, a clipped thick lawn, green
as a golf course, smooth footpaths, and neat little
English-speaking arrows directing mourners
to "Gramsci" and "W.C."

It's a relief to us Protestants, this orderly
plantation, yet even here Italian chaos
creeps over the fence: Where is the "Keats" sign?
worry the English ladies, fidgeting at the edge
of the ditch. The digger lays down his spade,

waves both hands toward the corner,
smile packed with intention, but does he intend
"Keats"? The ladies retreat into their sunhats,
nod wanly, then too vigorously, then hasten
precipitously into the shade, pretending to search

for Shelley. Only when my friend and I forge
boldly over the ditch and beeline a placid trio
of stones do the ladies brake and regress, politely
hovering with cameras while I examine the earth
for traces of violets (none) and consider

the fate of baby Severn, dead of an accident,
age one year. Another predestined blunder—
tipped out of a casement, choked on marzipan,
crushed by the cart of a fruit vendor . . .
My friend, a Sicilian Catholic from New Jersey,

amiably shouts, "Grazie!" at the digger,
who murmurs, "Prego, prego," and eyes her tits.
It's our last day in Rome, and she is humoring me,
killing time with dead poets and babies
when we could be squatting on the hot

Pantheon steps devouring artichokes
and strawberries from a plastic bag.

She flits her false lashes knowingly
at the digger, shifts her brassy red
pocketbook to the other freckled shoulder;

and the fidgeting ladies, alarmed,
are nonetheless impressed by her sang-froid,
another trait of my hungry people—
this laborious, admiring fear of eros:
and it *is* lovely,

the digger's desire, my friend's frank
acknowledgment, though I, like the ladies,
blush and scuttle. Shelley, poor sap,
doing his Jim-Morrison dance all over town,
wasn't, at heart, much better off;

he had to invent a sort of faith transcending
faithlessness—a house of cards
that would have crushed him in the end,
if the gulf hadn't eaten him first. The digger
commences his whistle, my friend and I recede,

the ladies, shy as ducks, open their *Portable
Romantics* and murmur a brief hymn;
the short lady sighs and closes her damp eyes:
all praise, they sing, to Keats,
bright star, alone and palely loitering.

Dying, you came staggering to Rome to live,
choking on black phlegm and gore,
dim eyes fixed on a gaudy sky.
And left behind your tired epitaph.
Nothing we make will matter.

Here it idles, scratched into the mossy
opalescent damp, embroidered with a passel
of lament you didn't want to hear.
But too little is never enough for our people,
once we've been jolted to love;

and I know baby Severn's father loved you,
dragging his nursemaid bones
down to the city limits sixty years later,
waiting out Judgment Day with you
and his child in arms, under the noon

jangle of a dozen Holy Roman church bells,
trams hissing to a stop, digger whistling an unknown
tune, my friend crossing herself, tendering
a muttered prayer for her cancer-mangled breast.
I'd light a candle, my brothers, if that were our way.

There's no denying him

announced the old lady at Bud's Shop 'n Save,
        grabbing your father's coat sleeve, eyeing you
up and down like post-office criminals.
        Flat cheekbones, shock of hair, same aloof,
thin-hipped stride, same touch-me-not scowl:
        six years old, already the masked man.
What have I done to deserve lover and son
        so beautiful, both remote as trout in green shallows?
I fritter my squirrel antics on the bank, swing
        head-first from a cedar bough: Notice me, notice me!
You cock his cool stare and flit into shadow, my slippery fish.
        But dangle the lure, the words—
up you flash, sun bronzing your quick scales.
        "Away went Alice like the wind!" you cry; "In *Lear* I love
the Fool!"
Feathers sprout from my worldly paws, your gills suckle air.
        New born, we flee open-eyed into the east,
bright wingbeats carving cloud, below us the unfolding sea—
        white chop, clean spray.
You know the story.

April

We smoke the roach you sweet-talked
crabby Lauren into parting with,
you drop ash in my hair, on the wall Joe Strummer

smashes a guitar, slow-hand Chaucer nudges my lips—
      . . . than longen folk to goon . . .
We're not exactly tripping any more, but streetlights

still flash their porous rainbows, the soft windows tremble and
      sigh,
and when you shake *Revolver* onto the turntable,
"She Said She Said" fattens the night air like a tulip.

      . . . the tendre croppes, the yonge sonne . . .
Already I'm afraid to leave you, already I'm lonely.
Eye-jangled and forlorn, I watch you rattle cellophane,

tear open a pack of Marlboros, cough and strike a match,
suck up the fumes of one more cigarette.
      . . . Zephirus eek with his sweete breeth . . .

The tulip sways. She bows low, she offers me her red throat.
      . . . so priketh him nature in hir corages . . .
What hurt, what hunger do I dread?

Convalescent

Bright morning in a garden chair
on the esplanade, mummified, half-prone,
amid shawls and thick rugs,
pleased to watch the steady wavelets

chink among the stones of the shingle,
the rain-dark weed; couples sprinkled
athwart the *plage* in rational pairings,
small ones crouched at the margin

of the tongued sea, white-frocked mothers
paused above them, parasols bowing
under the clean wind like cormorants.
And we helpless, not unhappy ones

also take the air—infants, fragile parents,
consumptive collectors of nature—
our rôle in the seaside schema clear
as looking-glass to any novelist

or digging child: we are the audience,
safely tucked beyond a cavernous
proscenium: no change, no dénouement;
our part mere endless, watchful pause.

Even I could pencil volumes in the room
of this eternal morning, placid time arrested,
every actor idle now, except my wife.
Fifty paces lonely, down the gravel walk,

she ducks the crown of her hat
gravely into wind—so thin, so spare,
yet she presses forward and away,
eager ship bound for passage,

fruit of the Indies sweet as her mind's eye,
though her only voyage is this solitary
foray to the jetty, servant of wind and salt,
gull-compass, adrift in the northern sea.

How simply she recedes.
A gust lifts the hem of her dress: and half
my heart cries desolation,
half croons its own brief hymn to solitude.

Even ardent sentinels require space
for love, a narrowed lens,
each elastic link of habit tense
and re-invigoured by our loneliness.

Tide splinters over pebbles, a rampant gust
seizes heedless gulls; the mothers on the beach
cling to parasols; and on the esplanade,
we invalids rustle in our chairs,

alarmed by autumn's deadly kiss.
Far down the jetty, my doll-wife pauses,
then turns, landward, hands to her hat,
brim bent, dark ribbons flying.

Now is the season of departure,
rich kick of wings into the east wind,

an avian ecstasy of sinew and speed.
Nothing seems less likely than return,

and yet her lips shape a query.
What rights have the earthbound
to answer nay? I raise my book aloft,
air drums between us like a harp-string,

and she begins to laugh, one glove
clutching her hat, the other
her fluttered skirt: the wind tears
at her hair; and laughing still,

she flings up both hands to me,
to the gull-current, sky
awash with ribbons, with silk;
and she runs.

Trouble

From the barren hills a battery of men
marched and stumbled onto the muddy plain,
but the wolves, impatient for spring, mistook them
for scrawny oxen and devoured them. Now the women,
no longer the wives of heroes, hoard turnips and spoiled
      loaves.
Mice gnaw the empty shelves, grind their yellow teeth
against the split handles of knives and hatchets.
Children launch greening potatoes at the anxious
cattle; they throttle the last angry geese. Pale sheep wander
the bleak forest like ragged deer, tearing twigs and blackened
leaves from the stunted oaks. A sallow pair of lambs huddles
by the half-thawed pool, where a single ancient fish lives out
his cloudy hours, calm, unfixed, a pitcher of silver and lead.
At dusk he drifts into the net.

Christmas at the Ramada

1. The Lobby

Ramada nearly rhymes with armada
a disarming coincidence, O notes,
as she shoves apart the glass doors

for lingering K and they step into
a Wonderland of holiday cheer
so cheerless she pictures just how hard

the squirrel-faced girl at the front desk
must have laughed when, the day
after Thanksgiving, a burly crew

of Portuguese teens crammed the pale
lobby with misshapen Edwardian carolers
and a giant twitching Santa with a gold-

lamé belt and a broken nose. Across the grubby
carpet, two mechanical elves lugubriously
negotiate a seesaw; the check-in counter

is bestrewn with large rats sporting Mr. and Mrs.
Claus outfits; and toward the lounge, a pair
of handyman snowmen wash and sweep

with the enthusiasm of wind-up convicts.
"Ramada/armada, ramada/armada,"

murmurs O. The air is lightly filled
with the tones of Christmas carols
so faint they might be the rustling
of bat wings. The lobby smells of dust

and industrial rug shampoo.
Beyond the night-time glass, asphalt looms.
The lights of Route 6 tout good prices

and fun. Cars stuffed with after-dinner
shoppers mutter past, tires scraping sand,
satisfaction imminent as a blizzard. O signs up

for a smoking room, a king-sized bed. K thumbs
postcards and examines a rat. In their veins,
the spirit of Christmas surges like bourbon.

   2. The Lounge

The lounge is respectably dim,
decked out with "old" posters
and swags of plastic fir, all its little

tables and vinyl benches clustered
TV-wise. Behind the bar a lady
with the gravelly bark of a classic-

rock DJ forks over a syrupy cocktail
and returns her gaze to the televised
town meeting currently mesmerizing

herself and her five retired fat-guy
customers, and now K and O, requesting
beer. Happy O rubs a shoulder into K's,

public-access TV displays a local
fiend in chairwoman's clothing
shouting wild threats at the fire chief,

and everyone in the room sighs with pleasure.
Pouring out K's Sam Adams, the bartender
cries huskily, "She's so *mean!*"

Her Santa hat jiggles in sympathy.
Through the frosted window glass,
emergency vehicles in the parking lot

flash red, white, and blue like a friendly
disco ball; and down the gilt bar a bug-eyed man
in a pressed shirt catches sight of his mirror self.

He turns to O and K, he leans toward O,
eager as a schoolboy, and marvels,
"Hey. I look really nice."

   3. The Bed

It lurks round every Ramada corner,
this bed, single-minded as Sparta.
Once the door chunks shut behind them,

once they inspect all the drawers and snigger
at the Oriental-ish art screwed
to the beige wallpaper, once they suck down

a quick roach at the icy casement,
time runs out for everything but the bed
and K and O—the gravitational pull

of this motel mattress, Charlemagne-
sized, its flowered coverlet severe;
a bed royally firm yet dim as a cave

in the shadow of the light fixtures.
Sex is the heart of the matter:
and perhaps, thinks O,

there is something vital in ugliness,
this reduction to famine,
we two thrown together like phantom

Barbarellas, and all the while the ice machine
crashes in the hall, handyman snowmen
whirr and clack, the fat guys in the lounge

switch to Friars hockey and whiskey sours,
and a tow truck finally drags a smashed-up
Chevy from the parking lot.

In the distance, a siren.
K leans back against the somber headboard,
silken and shy, open-eyed.

What magic to be awaited by a man
whose every rib she must have kissed
at least once in the half-life

they've dreamed away.
Though this bed demands a new,
a starker obeisance—

This stripped-down polyester
battlement, this outcast star—
No shepherd awake to guard his ewe lamb.

4. The TV

It's been Christmas at the Vatican
for hours already; but midnight mass
flickers into their ten P.M. motel room

like an accident. What's more,
the announcer is busily translating
every Latin phrase into rich

and obfuscating Spanish.
The pope looks terrible.
Under his golden robes and mitre,

he sags to one side like a cat
stuffed into fancy pajamas.
The camera can hardly bear to film him;

it keeps switching to a chanting
Salvadoran priest, dark and beautiful,
voice a thin angelic tenor,

though he is horribly nervous,
his shadowy chin trembling
between each honeyed line.

At home in San Salvador, his mother
is prostrate with fear of God,
O thinks, pressing her cheek into K's

bare arm. Now the camera shifts
to pan a row of old ladies draped in black
furry coats and orange lipstick;

they glare, outraged;
they look exactly like the old ladies
who instigate fender benders

on Elmwood Avenue, carelessly shooting
homeward after a day spent
plotting dominion; yet thank Heaven,

they're also the sentimental type
who adore enchanting priests.
How good of the holy church

to meet their needs with such pity
and take the heat off this poor pope
slumping unfilmed beneath his foreign

vault, his cold sky, a few brisk lights
scattered across the black. Not far off,
the faithful sleep, safe as milk.

Ethics, a Lament

One floor down, the washing machine
　　groans, churning its grey clot of socks
　　　　and tattered underwear; the well pump

clanks in tandem, sucks up another icy load
　　from its stony subterra chamber
　　　　echoing with clicks and rumbled machinations;

and at every slurping surge, earthworms thrust blind,
　　timorous snouts skyward into the tangled sod.
　　　　Just the dumb-ass fear a greedy robin craves.

He cocks a marble eye, then spears a flaccid twister,
　　flaps into the lilac hedge, graceless as a wingéd egg.
　　　　The burr-encrusted poodle peels out after him,

lurching like a Keystone Kop into a shrub; and what strikes me,
　　squinting at the action through my sun-licked window,
　　　　is Nature's clumsy avarice:

worms, Kops, and rusty washers junking up her cosmic
　　rat hole with rest of us haphazard, ratcheting souls.
　　　　"Eat or be eaten," I remark

fatuously to the bacon thawing on the counter,
　　a pig I met in springtime, under the apple tree,
　　　　feathered in satin petals and crunching up beetles.

Have mercy!— Is nothing straightforward in this life?

Even crushed beetles trundle their scratchy track toward
     heaven;
          bacon flounces into a dialectic sulk; the morality of
               water

bubbles under my landlocked feet; in the rickety barn
     three fat goats are rioting for grain;
          and what to do with these terrible socks,

two black heels rubbed down to mesh,
     but ball them up and toss them into the drawer.
          Christ, it's all out of my hands.

Sleep

I flaunt my silk underwear,
one more slit-eyed bitch
clogging your cracked headlights.
Any old hag is the girl of your dreams,

and I
am only halfway down the road to rot,
thumb-bone flagging your sleek
Cadillac.

Dust blunders at loose ends,
tornado blue, thick as brains.
I slouch ditch-side,
time's cynic.

Driver, don't make me wait.
Just hit,
hit, and run.

Notes & Acknowledgments

My love to Paul for loaning me his title; to James for his pride and his patience; to Tom who considers, always, how our light is spent.

As ever, I am indebted to Baron Wormser. I'm grateful as well for the advice and encouragement of Jeanne Marie Beaumont, Ellen Dudley, Meg Kearney, Howard Levy, David Moreau, Janice Potter, Weslea Sidon, and Janet Wormser. Thanks also to Jeffrey Haste at Deerbrook Editions for spurring my eclogue project and to Angela DeRosa, Ray Gish, and Donna Miller, who don't care whether or not I write poems but insist on talking to me about what matters in this life.

I had the good fortune to travel to Rome while working on this collection, thanks in part to a grant from the Maine Arts Commission, an independent state agency supported by the National Endowment for the Arts. But the heart of my voyage was Jilline Ringle. Our Roman holiday may be over, but she is forever my comrade and my beacon.

The opening epigraph quotes from Dumas, *The Count of Monte Cristo,* as translated in *Familiar Quotations,* 11th ed., by John Bartlett, ed. Christopher Morley (Little, Brown, 1939), 1067. Part I's Santayana epigraph is quoted in Edgar Johnson, *Charles Dickens: His Tragedy and Triumph* (Simon & Schuster, 1952), 2:1139. "National Emergency" quotes liberally from Cotton Mather's *The Wonders of the Invisible World* (1692) but inaccurately and out of context; see Mather, *On Witchcraft* (Dover, 2005), if you want the real thing. The Virgil quotation before my Eclogue I is from his Eclogue II (37 B.C.), in *The Eclogues,* trans. Guy Lee (Penguin, 1984), 41.

The first four lines of "Substitute Teacher" are Elizabeth Bowen's, from *The House in Paris* (1935; reprint, Penguin, 1987), 90. The Forster epigraph in "Cornville" is from *A Passage to India* (Harcourt, Brace & World, 1924), 277. "Peter Walsh" borrows his name from a character in Virginia Woolf's *Mrs. Dalloway* but is otherwise my own invention.

Part III's Milton epigraph is from the Merritt Y. Hughes edition of *Paradise Lost* (Odyssey, 1962), 13. Part IV's Graves epigraph appears in *The Greek Myths* (Penguin, 1955), 1:150. The quotation before "Protestant Cemetery" is the epitaph Keats composed for his gravestone, just before his death in 1821; and the quotation in the first stanza paraphrases an early verse letter, cited in W. Jackson Bate, *John Keats* (Belknap/Harvard University Press, 1964), 34. The Chaucer lines in "April" are from the General Prologue of *The Canterbury Tales* (ca. 1386), in *The Complete Poetry and Prose of Geoffrey Chaucer,* ed. John H. Fisher (Holt, Rinehart, & Winston, 1977), 9-10. Finally, "Trouble" incorporates all twenty words on one of my son's third-grade spelling lists.

I am grateful to the editors of the following journals for publishing my poems:

> *Animus:* "Why I Didn't Finish Reading *David Copperfield*"
> *Antioch Review:* "Ethics, a Lament"
> *Ars Interpres:* "Madrigal"
> *Bangor Metro:* "Litany for J"
> *Beloit Poetry Journal:* "Peter Walsh," "Touching"
> *Blue Collar Review:* Eclogue II
> *Café Review:* "Radio Song"
> *Connecticut Review:* "Convalescent"

Interpoezia: "Christmas at the Ramada," Eclogues III
and IV, "Rumpelstiltskin's Garden"
Marlboro Review: "Aubade"
Off the Coast: Eclogue I, "The Master"
Prairie Schooner: "Exile"
Puckerbrush Review: "Protestant Cemetery," "There's no
denying him"
roger: "First Game"
Sakana: "Don't be afraid to"
Salamander: "April," "Burglar"

"Heavy Metal" appears in the teaching materials of *Bridging
English* (4th ed.), by Joseph Milner and Lucy Milner (Upper
Saddle River, N.J.: Merrill/Prentice Hall, 2007). Eclogue I
and "Rumpelstiltskin's Garden" were reprinted in the 2006
Fedco seed catalog, and I planted my garden on the proceeds.
Eclogue II was a finalist for the 2005 Robert Frost Foundation
Poetry Award. "Peter Walsh" was nominated for a 2008
Pushcart Prize.

Dawn Potter is associate director of the Frost Place Conference on Poetry and Teaching. Her most recent book is a memoir, *Tracing Paradise: Two Years in Harmony with John Milton* (University of Massachusetts Press, 2009). She has also published a previous poetry collection, *Boy Land & Other Poems* (Deerbrook Editions, 2004). She lives in Harmony, Maine, with photographer Thomas Birtwistle and their two sons.

CavanKerry's Mission

Through publishing and programming, CavanKerry Press
connects communities of writers with communities of readers.
We publish poetry that reaches from the page to include the
reader, by the finest new and established contemporary writers.
Our programming brings our books and our poets to people
where they live, cultivating new audiences and nourishing
established ones.

Other Books in the Notable Voices Series

CavanKerry now uses only recycled paper in its book production. Printing this book on 30% PCW and FSC certified paper saved 2 trees, 1 million BTUs of energy, 127 lbs. of CO_2, 67 lbs. of solid waste, and 524 gallons of water.